# BRITAIN IN OLD PHOTOGRAPHS

# CAMBERWELL, DULWICH & PECKHAM

## STEPHEN HUMPHREY

SUTTON PUBLISHING LIMITED

Sutton Publishing Limited
Phoenix Mill · Thrupp · Stroud
Gloucestershire · GL5 2BU

First published 1996

Copyright © Stephen Humphrey, 1996

Cover photographs. Front: Camberwell Green, 20 July 1909 (*see* p. 124). Back: works outing, A.T. Gadsby Ltd, 1922 (*see* p. 44)

**British Library Cataloguing in Publication Data**
A catalogue record for this book is available from the British Library.

ISBN 0-7509-1098-4

Typeset in 10/12 Perpetua.
Typesetting and origination by
Sutton Publishing Limited.
Printed in Great Britain by
Ebenezer Baylis, Worcester

# CONTENTS

| | | |
|---|---|---|
| | Introduction | 5 |
| 1. | Municipal Camberwell | 7 |
| 2. | Camberwell Green | 15 |
| 3. | Camberwell Grove and Grove Lane | 23 |
| 4. | North Camberwell | 29 |
| 5. | The Surrey Canal | 33 |
| 6. | Industry and Commerce | 37 |
| 7. | Churches and Chapels | 45 |
| 8. | Schools | 53 |
| 9. | Parks | 59 |
| 10. | Libraries | 65 |
| 11. | Peckham | 69 |
| 12. | Shops in and around Rye Lane | 75 |
| 13. | Denmark Hill | 83 |
| 14. | North Dulwich and Herne Hill | 89 |
| 15. | Dulwich Village | 95 |
| 16. | East Dulwich | 105 |
| 17. | Nunhead and the Cemeteries | 111 |
| 18. | The World Wars | 115 |
| 19. | Royal Occasions | 121 |
| | Acknowledgements | 128 |

Part of the vast premises of Jones & Higgins Ltd in Rye Lane, the largest store in the district, which existed from 1867 to 1980. In 1907 there were 629 employees, of whom 311 lived in a hostel attached to the shop. By the 1920s 1,000 people worked for the store. See Section 12 for further pictures.

# INTRODUCTION

Camberwell, Dulwich and Peckham are districts which formed the Metropolitan Borough of Camberwell between 1900 and 1965 and which constituted the parish of St Giles, Camberwell, for centuries previously. Since 1965 they have belonged to the London Borough of Southwark. Camberwell and Peckham might appear to have been well within the built-up area of London for generations, but if you look at maps as relatively recent as the early nineteenth century, you will see that they were then on the furthest fringe of London. The entire parish had just 7,059 people in 1801. It was possible at that time to see the red-winged Camberwell Beauty butterfly, which was a mark of a rural district. Today, despite its absence, it remains a well known local symbol. Dulwich has developed far less densely than Camberwell and Peckham and still retains much open space; the development which has taken place there is largely more recent than that in the area's northern neighbours. Dulwich could claim to have been still a hamlet for some decades after Camberwell and Peckham had become fully fledged suburbs.

Camberwell's transformation from country village to Georgian suburb depended on changes in transport and communications. Until 1750 there was only one bridge across the Thames in central London – Old London Bridge – and consequently the south side of the river was undeveloped beyond the town of Southwark and the river front itself. The opening of Westminster Bridge in 1750 and Blackfriars Bridge in 1769, together with the building of new roads to serve them and the gradual improvement of older routes, prompted much building. A turnpike trust took over the old road from the Elephant and Castle to Camberwell Green in 1782, and along that route – Walworth Road and Camberwell Road – Georgian terraces appeared before the end of the century. Similar terraces were built in the Old Kent Road. Near the old centres of Camberwell and Peckham, and in Peckham Road between the two, some grander houses were built. In the early nineteenth century, the building of more new bridges – Waterloo, Southwark and Vauxhall – increased the pace of development. Camberwell New Road was laid out to connect with Vauxhall Bridge, and made the route from New Cross through Peckham and Camberwell as busy as the traditional entry to London via the Old Kent Road. The building of Camberwell New Road is still roughly dated by the presence of the King William IV public house; he reigned from 1830 to 1837.

Further development later in the ninteenth century, particularly in East Dulwich, was encouraged firstly by the building of railways and then by the introduction of horse-drawn trams. The London, Chatham and Dover Railway was the first line to be built near the old heart of Camberwell, in 1862. Originally, there was a station in Camberwell New Road (still recalled by Camberwell Station Road) but it was closed in 1916. The best surviving Victorian station is the one at Denmark Hill, dating from 1866 and finely restored in recent years. Peckham has a distinguished place in the history of public transport in London, for it was the headquarters of Thomas Tilling, who ran the best known horse-drawn bus route in the capital from 1851. In 1904 his firm ran the first service to use double-deck motor buses in permanent replacement of horse-drawn vehicles in central London.

The low-lying northern end of Camberwell was much affected by the building of the Surrey Canal between 1801 and 1826. A route of 3½ miles from Rotherhithe to Camberwell Road was completed in 1811, and the Peckham branch, at right angles to it, was opened fifteen years later. The canal was connected to the Surrey Docks at Rotherhithe, which formed the centre of London's timber trade, and so the canal was lined with many timber yards. It also attracted works which produced cement, tar, whiting and mineral waters; at one time no fewer than four factories producing mineral waters stood near the canal. Another nearby factory, which belonged to Watkins, Watkins & Co. Ltd, bound up to one million Bibles a year for the British and Foreign Bible Society.

For Church purposes, the whole of Camberwell, Dulwich and Peckham constituted the single parish of St Giles, Camberwell until the nineteenth century. Old St Giles's Church was burnt down in 1841 and was replaced in 1842–4 by the present building, designed by Sir Gilbert Scott. A church fit for a proud and prosperous suburb had replaced a small and ancient village church. By that time daughter churches had been built. The most prominent of them was St George's, which was built in Greek Classical style next to the Surrey Canal in 1822–4. The oldest was Christ's Chapel at Dulwich, which was consecrated in 1616 to serve Edward Alleyn's foundation. By the end of the nineteenth century several dozen churches of various denominations stood within the ancient boundaries of St Giles's parish.

The photographs in this book date largely from the first third of this century. They show the culmination of a century of development and expansion which made Camberwell a town of more than a quarter of a million people. Much of what you see here has been made unfamiliar by the drastic architectural, social and economic changes which have transformed the area since 1939. These pictures therefore serve as an introduction to the modern history of a significant part of London.

# MUNICIPAL
# CAMBERWELL

*Camberwell Town Hall, as remodelled in 1934.
E.G. Culpin and R.S. Bowers designed the encasing and
extension of the earlier building. The details on the front
are in Portland stone.*

Camberwell Borough Council meeting in the remodelled town hall, 10 October 1934. The mayor was Councillor S. Ernest Hall. The pennant or standard displayed above him was made at the Camberwell School of Arts and Crafts to incorporate a badge granted by the College of Arms in 1927.

The old Camberwell Town Hall, *c.* 1925. It had been built in 1872–3 as the Vestry Hall of St Giles's Parish. Edward Power was its architect. The borough council superseded the vestry in 1900. The turret clock, which was supplied by Alexander Dalgety of Peckham, was flanked by figures representing Law, Justice and Prudence.

Alderman J.W.F. Lucas, Mayor of Camberwell in 1934–5 and 1954–5. Lucas Gardens in Peckham Road were named after him. The mace seen here was presented by local licensed victuallers in 1918.

An open-air art exhibition held at Camberwell Green from 22 May to 3 June 1950, to mark the Golden Jubilee of the Metropolitan Borough of Camberwell.

Pensioners of the Vestry of St Giles's Parish, 1899. The vestry was superseded by Camberwell Borough Council in the following year.

The laying of the foundation stone of the Grove Vale Depot by Edwin Robert Phillips, Chairman of Camberwell Vestry, 8 September 1900. The site of 1¼ acres was laid out under the supervision of the Vestry's engineer, W. Oxtoby, and included accommodation for eighty-eight horses.

Camberwell Borough Council Officers' dinner, 12 November 1901. The mayor was W. Scott-Scott.

The teams in the cricket match between Camberwell and Hastings, on 6 July 1907. The game was played because Camberwell's town clerk, Charles William Tagg, lived in Hastings. Camberwell's team made 122 and then bowled out Hastings for 74, all ten wickets being taken by S. W. Thompson.

The South London Art Gallery (right) and the Camberwell School of Arts and Crafts (left), *c*. 1900, two important local institutions founded in Peckham Road in the 1890s. The gallery originated in Blackfriars Road in Southwark in 1868 under the leadership of William Rossiter. In 1889 he bought Portland House in Peckham Road, and between then and 1898 the gallery grew to its full size. The school of art was opened in 1898 'in order to provide instruction in those branches of design and manipulation which directly bear on the more artistic trades'.

Food from Camberwell in Victoria, Australia, sent as a Christmas gift in 1948, in the still-rationed years after the Second World War.

The North Camberwell Baths, Old Kent Road (on the left), *c.* 1920. They cost £70,000 to build, and opened in 1905.

# CAMBERWELL
# GREEN

*Camberwell Green in 1906, in a view looking towards Camberwell Church Street.*

The old police station at Camberwell Green, on the corner of Camberwell New Road, *c.* 1890. The building was demolished in 1898 and a bank took its place (see below).

The bank building, constructed on the site of the old police station. It has been Camberwell Green's main landmark throughout this century.

A Christmas card, *c.* 1910, showing the houses on the east side of Camberwell Green, which were demolished soon afterwards to make way for a Peabody estate. The Greencoat School can be seen in the background.

Surviving buildings of the Greencoat School on the north side of Camberwell Green, 1956. The school was founded in 1706 and was rebuilt on this site in 1871. It was merged with Wilson's Grammar School after the Second World War.

Lowth Road, off Coldharbour Lane near Camberwell Green, *c.* 1910.

The London County Council's trams' office, 301–3 Camberwell New Road, 1908. Electric trams ran in the area from 1903 to 1952.

Residents of Tiger Yard, at the foot of Denmark Hill, 1934. The Tiger public house became the Silver Buckle.

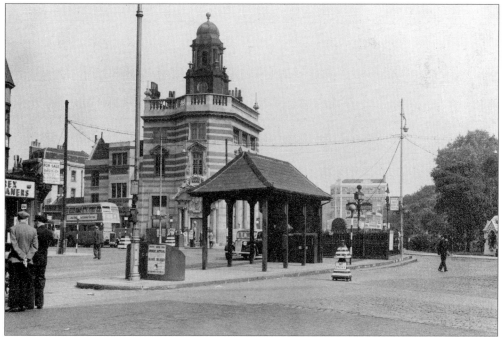

Camberwell Green, 1952.

A view from the foot of Denmark Hill towards Camberwell Church Street, *c.* 1912. Electric trams, as seen here, were introduced in 1903.

Camberwell Church Street, *c.* 1905. This route became busier when Camberwell New Road and Vauxhall Bridge were built in the early nineteenth century.

George Edward Waller's boot warehouse, 29 Camberwell Church Street, *c.* 1895. The large hanging lamps were typical fixtures on turn-of-the-century shops and pubs, used to illuminate the façades on dark evenings in dimly lit streets.

Camberwell Baths, off Camberwell Church Street, *c.* 1895. The baths cost nearly £41,000 to build and opened in 1892. The building was designed by Messrs Spalding and Cross, who also designed Dulwich Baths (*see* page 110).

# CAMBERWELL GROVE
# AND
# GROVE LANE

*Grove Lane, c. 1900.*

View of Camberwell from the Grove, 1776, taken from Walter Harrison's *Universal History, Description and Survey of London, Westminster and Southwark*. The arcaded building on the left, dating from 1748, was the Grove House Tavern. It became Camberwell Hall, a principal venue for meetings. It still stands today, as No. 45 Grove Lane. On the right of the picture is old St Giles's Church, which was burnt down in 1841 and replaced by the building shown on page 48. The Grove was a landscaped walk in 1776, leading from the back of the manor house in Camberwell Church Street, shown here in the centre background, framed by the trees.

Camberwell Grove, looking south, *c.* 1912. The Grove House Tavern is on the right. It was rebuilt in the 1930s.

A view from the same position as above, but looking north towards Camberwell Church Street.

Grove Crescent, 1836. These houses had been built in 1819 for William Whitton on land which had previously belonged to Dr John Coakley Lettsom. They still stand today towards the south end of Camberwell Grove. No other houses have ever stood on that land. In Lettsom's day, the land formed part of Upper Springfield. He had bought the estate in 1779 and built his mansion, Grove Hill, further up the hill, in what is now Park Grove.

Thatched cottage, Camberwell Grove, early in the twentieth century.

Old stables in Camberwell Grove, *c.* 1905.

Grove Lane, near the summit of the hill, *c*. 1880.

Grove Lane, *c*. 1900.

# NORTH
# CAMBERWELL

*A copy of the watercolour painted by Frank Adams of Walworth Road for the Valentine Comic Postcard series. The famous coster song, 'Knocked 'em in the Old Kent Road', featured a couple who had inherited a donkey shay from 'rich Uncle Tom of Camberwell'.*

Southampton Street (now Southampton Way), *c.* 1910. The Crescent Arms public house is on the left.

A women's outing group outside the Crescent Arms in mid-century.

St George's Road in Edwardian days. This street ran parallel with the Surrey Canal on the canal's south side.

Albany Chapel, photographed prior to demolition in March 1887. It had been built for an independent congregation in the early nineteenth century. The street in which it stood, Albany Road, had been named after the Duke of York and Albany ('the grand old Duke of York').

New Church Road, *c.* 1905. The taller building on the left was the Trinity College Mission, founded in 1885. Evelina Mansions stand on the right.

A view across the rooftops of the Sultan Street area, to the west of Camberwell Road, which was considered a dreadful slum in 1939, when this picture was taken. The spire in the distance is that of St John the Divine in Vassall Road.

# THE SURREY CANAL

*Boys fishing in the canal, c. 1920.*

The canal in a view looking east towards St George's Church and the Wells Way bridge, *c*. 1925. A sailing barge dominates the foreground. This was the westernmost part of the canal, which opened in 1811 and was the brainchild of Ralph Dodd. The church was built in 1822–4 to Francis Bedford's designs. The low, gabled building in front of it on the canal side was the parochial school, built in 1839–40 by W.G. Colman.

A very similar view as in the preceding picture, but taken from a position nearer to the bridge.

Canal Head at Peckham, *c.* 1930. This branch of the canal, which ran at a right angle to the main section, was completed in 1826. The tower of Jones & Higgins at the junction of Peckham High Street and Rye Lane dominates the background.

A scene 'upstream' of Canal Bridge, Old Kent Road, *c.* 1930. On the right there were a large municipal dust shoot and, nearer the camera, Acorn Wharf, the extensive premises of R. May & Son Ltd, timber merchants. The wharf was established in 1855.

The same location as in the preceding picture, but looking west ('upstream') rather than east. The dust shoot is on the left.

# INDUSTRY
# AND
# COMMERCE

*The South Metropolitan Gas Works, Old Kent Road, c. 1910. The company had been founded in 1829 and took over this site in 1832.*

An outing from the gas works.

Christ Church was first built on the north side of Old Kent Road in 1837–8 to Samuel Angell's designs. Under an Act of 1865, it was bought by the South Metropolitan Gas Company which demolished it and replaced it by a retort house. A new church was built across the road in 1867–8 by E. Bassett Keeling.

A Tilling's bus in Rye Lane, *c.* 1900. Thomas Tilling ran a regular horse-bus service between Peckham and the West End from 1851 and was the first to introduce double-deck motor buses to central London in 1904. The Milnes Daimler was the first motor bus the firm used.

Tilling's staff at the Bull Yard depot, Peckham, between the wars. This was the firm's first depot for motor buses.

The 'Bible factory' of Watkins, Watkins & Co. Ltd of Cowan Street, near Albany Road, possibly *c*. 1930. The firm bound Bibles for the British and Foreign Bible Society.

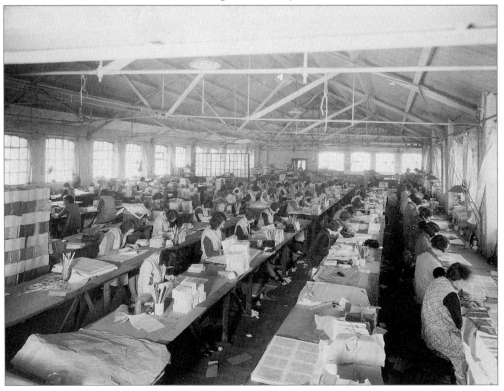

Women working in the Bible factory.

James Banks's butcher's shop, 8 Waterloo Street (now Elmington Road), *c.* 1910.

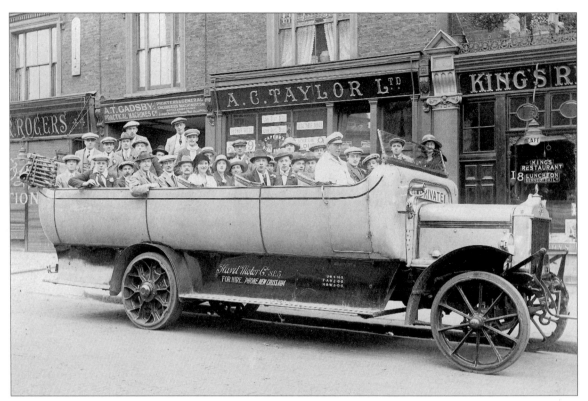

An outing from the firm of A.T. Gadsby Ltd, photographed outside the firm's premises at 42a Denmark Hill in 1922. Gadsby's also owned the St George's Engineering Works in Waterloo Street (now Elmington Road). The firm made machinery for the printing and allied trades.

Staff of Heinz & Co.'s factory at Peckham, June 1922. The firm had taken over an old-established pickle manufacturer, Batty & Co. of 127 Brayards Road, thereby acquiring its first factory in England.

Staff at Mansons Ltd, transport maintenance engineers of Ingoldisthorpe Grove, Glengall Road, between the wars, photographed by H. Bown, snr.

A milk float belonging to R. Higgs & Sons, a firm which had numerous premises throughout Camberwell.

# CHURCHES
# AND
# CHAPELS

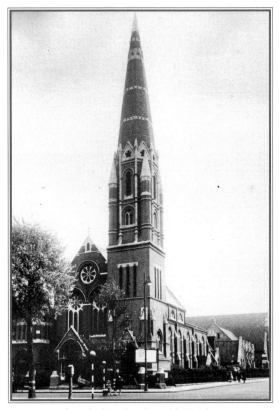

*Barry Road Methodist Church, c. 1950. This impressive church, built in 1873–4 to Charles Bell's designs, stood at the junction of Barry Road and Upland Road until 1965. The congregation now forms part of Christ Church, which meets in a building next to the former Emmanuel Church at the Lordship Lane end of Barry Road.*

The mother church of Camberwell is that of St Giles in Camberwell Church Street. The present building dates from 1842–4 and was designed by Sir Gilbert Scott. It ranks as a significant work from the early years of the Gothic Revival. Its style is that of the thirteenth century. John Ruskin, who lived at Denmark Hill, helped to design the east window, which was made by the firm of Ward & Nixon. A church has stood on the site since at least 1086.

Emmanuel Church in Camberwell Road, seen here in 1963, was built in 1841–2 and cost £4,899. Thomas Bellamy was its architect. It may have been the church which Charles Dickens had in mind when Mr Wemmick married Miss Skiffins. The building was closed in 1963.

The imposing church of St Matthew in Denmark Hill was built in 1848. A.D. Gough was its architect. The church was destroyed by bombing in the Second World War and its site was later used for the dental section of King's College Hospital.

Camden Church in Peckham Road was opened in 1797 for a congregation of the Countess of Huntingdon's Connexion. It became an Anglican chapel of ease in 1829 and a full parish church in 1844. Henry Melvill (*see* below) was its distinguished minister from 1829 to 1844. The building was destroyed by bombing in the Second World War.

Henry Melvill, minister of Camden Chapel,
depicted here in an engraving by J.J. Williams,
*c*. 1832.

St Chrysostom's Church in Peckham Hill Street, *c.* 1920. It was built in 1813–14 and was demolished in 1963. For much of the nineteenth century it was privately owned. It was originally named Peckham Chapel and was renamed in 1865 after St John Chrysostom, Archbishop of Constantinople (347–407).

The interior of the Queen's Road Wesleyan Methodist church, Peckham, *c.* 1905. It had been built in 1864–5 to replace a building in Stafford (now Staffordshire) Street. The present Peckham Methodist Church of 1973–4 stands on part of its site.

The church of St John the Evangelist, Goose Green, seen here in a painting of *c*. 1865, probably by Philip A. Bosworth. The church was designed by Charles Baily and was built in 1863–5. J.B.S. Comper repaired it after damage in the Second World War.

St Clement's Church, Friern Road, East Dulwich, *c*. 1905. Designed by William B. Hughes, it was built in 1884–5. It was destroyed in 1940 and replaced by the present church.

Christ's Chapel in the Old College in Dulwich Village, *c.* 1920. The chapel was consecrated in 1616 as part of Edward Alleyn's College of God's Gift. The founder's tomb may be seen in the central aisle; he died in 1626.

The temporary iron church, *c.* 1875, for what became the parish of All Saints, Rosendale Road. The temporary church stood in Thurlow Park Road. Its permanent replacement was built in 1888–91.

The interior of St Paul's Church, Herne Hill, 1844. George Alexander designed the original church of 1843–4, but following a fire in 1858, it was extensively remodelled by G.E. Street.

# SCHOOLS

*A class at the Greencoat School, Camberwell Green, c. 1917. The school's buildings may be seen on page 19.*

Infants' class, Grove Lane School, *c.* 1909.

Infants' class, Oliver Goldsmith School, Peckham Road, *c.* 1920.

Oliver Goldsmith School, Peckham Road, *c.* 1905. The road to the right is Southampton Street (now Southampton Way). In the background, to the right of the nearer tram, Camden Church may be seen (*See* page 50). The school was one of the many built by the London School Board, which usually towered over their neighbours in late Victorian days.

Form II at Peckham Central School, 1926. Central Schools offered a more substantial education than the ordinary elementary schools between the wars.

James Allen's Girls' School, East Dulwich Grove, *c*. 1910. The school was founded by a Master of Dulwich College in 1741. It grew to its modern eminence when it reopened in these buildings in 1886.

South London School, Preparatory Department, 508 Lordship Lane, *c.* 1924. Ernest J.H. Marsland was the headmaster. He also appears in directories as a 'civil service tutor'.

Lyndhurst Road School, *c.* 1910.

Wilson's Grammar School, *c.* 1905. Founded by a vicar of St Giles's in 1615, this school stands on the opposite side of Wilson Road from the church. The school moved to Sutton in 1975.

A class at Oliver Goldsmith School, *c.* 1931.

# PARKS
# AND
# GARDENS

*The opening of One Tree Hill as a public open space, 7 August 1905. A golf club had enclosed the space in 1896, causing public agitation, leading to a near-riot in 1897. Camberwell Borough Council eventually bought the land for £6,100 from the owner, J.E. Ward. The hill is 345 ft high.*

The opening of Peckham Rye Park; 14 May 1894. The land, which had previously been used for farming, was bought for public recreation by the London County Council and other local authorities. Camberwell Vestry contributed £20,000. On the opening day, which was Whit Monday, a procession went from Camberwell Vestry Hall to the park. Trades Unions, friendly societies and temperance societies all took part; their banners can be seen in the picture. The vote of thanks to the Chairman of the London County Council, Mr John Hutton, was proposed by Edwin Jones, the proprietor of Jones & Higgins. He was also a member of London County Council.

Children at the entrance to Dulwich Park in Court Lane, *c.* 1910. The land for this park was given by the Estate Governors of Alleyn's foundation.

Dulwich Park, *c.* 1890, in a view looking across to the Old College. The tower is that of Christ's Chapel (*see* page 53).

The grounds of Camberwell House, 1934. The house served as a private mental asylum from 1846 to 1955. The grounds later became Lucas Gardens, a public park, named after the mayor pictured on page 10.

Sister Mabel's donkey parade in the grounds of Camberwell House, c. 1890.

The boating lake, Peckham Rye Park, *c*. 1900.

The Mayor of Camberwell, C.A.G. Manning, planting a tree in the North Camberwell Open Space, 31 December 1951. This decidedly bureaucratic name was applied to the beginnings of what is now Burgess Park. This planting came after the London County Council had given twenty-five trees to Camberwell Borough Council. In the background, to the left of the tree, is Freda Corbet, MP for Peckham.

Peckham Rye Park, *c.* 1910.

The lake and extensive private gardens of Bessemer House (*see also* page 91).

# LIBRARIES

Nunhead Library, Gordon Road, c. 1905. R.P. Whellock designed the building, which opened on
1 December 1896. The cost was a mere £4,784. The library was one of those given by
John Passmore Edwards.

Camberwell Central Library in Peckham Road, *c.* 1905. The building was designed by R.P. Whellock and opened in 1893. It was destroyed in the Second World War.

The corridor of Camberwell Central Library, photographed by Frederick G.S. Port. The corridor was 10 ft wide, 100 ft long, and contained granite columns and a mosaic pavement.

The opening of Peckham Hill Street Library on Saturday 24 March 1954. The Mayor is Councillor Miss Rosina Whyatt. On her left is Alderman Mrs Jessie Burgess, Chairman of the Libraries Committee, after whom Burgess Park was named. On her left is Mrs Freda Corbet, MP for Peckham. The Borough Librarian, Mr W.J.A. Hahn, stands at the extreme left.

The opening of the Music Library, Peckham Road, 30 November 1957. The Borough Librarian, Miss Grace Johnson, is showing a record to John Hollingsworth, Conductor of the Royal Opera, who undertook the formal opening.

The opening of a new wing at Dulwich Library on 25 September 1954 by the Mayor, Alderman Lucas (*see* page 10). The new wing, which included the hall seen here, replaced one which had been bombed in 1940.

Camberwell Libraries' service for the aged and infirm, 1951. The van is in Grove Hill Road.

# PECKHAM

*Queen's Road, c. 1910. The number of shops everywhere grew considerably towards the end of the nineteenth century and was at its peak in this period.*

Peckham High Street, looking east, *c.* 1910. The large, turreted building on the left is the Crown Theatre, opened in 1898. Ernest Runtz was its architect. In 1912 it became the Peckham Hippodrome cinema. In the distance is the spire of Queen's Road Wesleyan Methodist church (*see* page 51).

The junction of Rye Lane and Peckham High Street, *c.* 1895. The building on the right is Hanover Chapel, dating from 1817 but tracing its history back to 1657, when it was the meeting house of Meeting House Lane. It was an Independent or Congregational chapel.

Some of the herd of cows kept in Lugard Road, *c*. 1935. When this dairy closed in 1967 its owner, John Jorden, was a fourth-generation cowkeeper in Peckham. It was an extraordinary survival for such an urban area.

The Pioneer Health Centre, St Mary's Road, *c*. 1938. Dr Innes Pearse and Dr George Scott Williamson founded their project in 1926. The building in St Mary's Road was run by them from 1935 to 1939 and again from 1946 to 1950. Sir Owen Williams was the architect.

Sunbury, a house at Peckham Rye, 1871. One of the two girls standing to the right of the door is Elizabeth Taylor who married George Cadbury, the chocolate magnate, in 1898. She was born at Peckham Rye in 1858 and died in 1951, an honoured philanthropist.

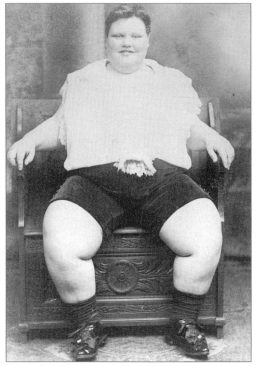

Johnny Trunley, *c*. 1909. He lived from 1898 to 1944 and weighed 33 stones at the age of 18. He attended Reddin's Road School at the same time as the writer Edgar Wallace. He spent much of his life on the stage and in films, but ended as a watch and clock maker in Gordon Road.

Peckham Rovers, *c.* 1900: a typical turn-of-the-century sporting group.

Peckham House, 1953. This private mental asylum was opened in 1826 in an eighteenth-century mansion, and survived until 1951. Warwick Park School now occupies the site.

# SHOPS
# IN AND AROUND
# RYE LANE

*The landmark building of Jones & Higgins Ltd dominates this view of the junction of Peckham High Street and Rye Lane at the turn of this century. To the left of the big building is the Kentish Drovers, one of Peckham's oldest pubs. It survived until 1954.*

George Randell Higgins (1844–1920) (left) and Edwin Jones (1837–1916) (right), who founded the famous drapery firm at 3 Rye Lane in 1867. The firm became a limited company in 1896 and remained independent until 1954. The store closed in 1980.

The junction of Peckham High Street and Rye Lane, 1889. Jones and Higgins later bought most of the property in the background and transformed this scene into that shown on page 77. In 1889 one shop was occupied by the shoe firm founded by Edward Harris Rabbits in 1846. Its headquarters were at the Elephant and Castle.

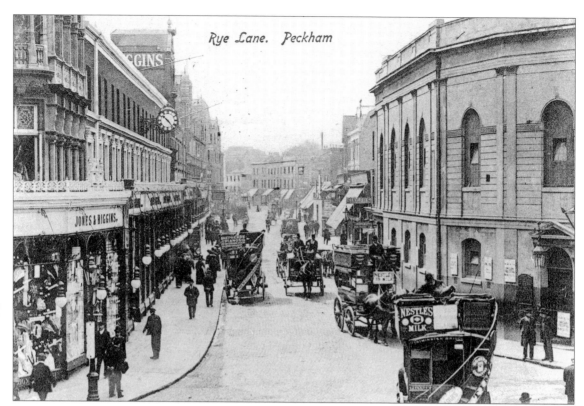

*Rye Lane. Peckham*

A view down Rye Lane, *c.* 1900. The premises of Jones & Higgins are on the left. The Hanover Chapel stands on the right (*see* page 73).

Part of Jones & Higgins's extensive frontage, 1953.

A branch of George Carter & Sons Ltd, 90–2 Rye Lane, *c.* 1927. The firm's main shop was at 211–17 Old Kent Road. At its centenary in 1951, the firm had twenty-five shops, including a second one in Rye Lane (at no. 131).

H. Holdron Ltd, *c.* 1927. This firm had considerable premises in Rye Lane (nos 117–25 and 135–47), including an arcade (*see* opposite).

Holdron's arcade, *c.* 1927.

A view from Bournemouth Road towards Rye Lane, *c.* 1927. Holdron's is on the right and the Tower Cinema in the background. The cinema was opened by Gladys Cooper on 19 November 1914 and closed in 1956. It was a landmark in the street.

Frank Smith's fruit shop at 24a Peckham Rye, *c.* 1908.

A shoe shop at 56 Victoria Road (now 73 Bellenden Road), probably before the First World War.

# DENMARK
# HILL

*The Camberwell Palace at 23–31 Denmark Hill, at the turn of the century. It was built in 1896 as the Oriental Palace of Varieties and was renamed in 1899. E.A.E. Woodrow was the architect.*

Denmark Hill, seen from the junction with Coldharbour Lane, 1889. A few years later the buildings in the foreground were replaced by the Metropole Theatre (*see* opposite). The spire in the distance is that of St Matthew's Church (*see* page 49).

The Camberwell Empire, 1907. The Metropole Theatre (*see* opposite) had been renamed in 1906.

The Metropole Theatre, *c*. 1900. It was built in 1894 to the designs of Bertie Crewe and W.G.R. Sprague. Live performances ceased in 1918. The building was demolished and replaced by an Odeon in 1937 (*see* next page).

The Odeon in 1954.

A queue outside the Odeon, 1956. Note how everyone is remarkably formal and conformist in dress.

Denmark Hill at the turn of the century.

Smith & Son, 120 Denmark Hill, *c.* 1906. It
consisted of a baker's and confectioner's, plus a
post office and telegraph office.

King's College Hospital, *c.* 1914. It had been built in 1909–13 on land given in 1904 by Lord Hambledon. This view shows the Bessemer Road frontage.

Twining Ward, King's College Hospital, 1916.

# NORTH DULWICH
# AND
# HERNE HILL

*The observatory on Sir Henry Bessemer's estate at North Dulwich, c. 1905. This view is in Green Dale, between East Dulwich Grove and Champion Hill. Sir Henry (1813–98) was the inventor of a process of making steel, and his estate, bought in 1863, boasted considerable grounds and a farm as well as this observatory.*

The drawing room of Bessemer's mansion, *c.* 1910. This property was called Bessemer House; nearby was Bessemer Grange (*see* opposite), which was built for Sir Henry's daughter. Both properties were demolished after the Second World War.

The exotic opulence of Bessemer's conservatory.

Bessemer Grange, seen from the south-east, *c.* 1922.

The old Half Moon Hotel at Herne Hill before demolition in 1896. Its replacement set the seal on the area's transformation from a rural road junction in the early nineteenth century to a respectable suburb of late Victorian and Edwardian times.

The Half Moon was built in 1898. This view is looking towards Half Moon Lane.

The Sunray Estate, Herne Hill, *c*. 1930. The estate was begun in 1920 and comprised 292 homes. It was a practical response to Lloyd George's cry, 'homes fit for heroes'.

The Herne Hill stadium in use for a cycle race, 1908.

A donkey parade at Herne Hill stadium.

# DULWICH VILLAGE

*Dulwich College, as built by Charles Barry Jnr, in College Road in 1870. Money paid by railway companies to run their lines across the college estate in the 1860s had financed these grand buildings.*

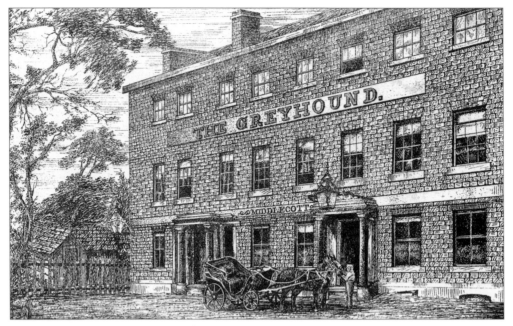

The Greyhound in Dulwich Village. This was the meeting-place of the Dulwich Club in the nineteenth century: Dickens, Thackeray and other eminent literary figures attended. The building was demolished in 1898 and a new Crown and Greyhound was built opposite, on the site of the previous Crown.

The Greyhound, *c.* 1890.

A Somerset House cricket team at the Greyhound, *c*. 1880.

A van belonging to William Bartley, fruiterer and florist of 29 Dulwich Village, *c*. 1920.

Bell House, College Road, 1952. The house was built in 1767 for Thomas Wright, a City Alderman.

Glenlea, Dulwich Common, 1952. The house was built by George Tappen for Charles Druce in 1804. From 1943 to 1945 it was leased by the Netherlands Government to train agents for operations in the occupied Netherlands.

Dulwich toll gate, College Road, at the turn of the century. Tolls were first charged here in 1789 by John Morgan, Lord of the Manor of Penge, who had rented some fields in Dulwich.

The other, much less familiar, toll gate in Dulwich, which stood in Court Lane.

Sir Evan Spicer, the paper magnate, who occupied Belair in Gallery Road until his death in 1938.

Belair in decay, October 1960. In the early 1960s the house was reconstructed and was shorn of its nineteenth-century additions. It had originally been built in 1785 for John Willes, and was called College Place. In 1967 the grounds served as the setting for the Dulwich Millenium Pageant.

An interior at the Grange, Grange Lane, c. 1900. The house was the home of Commander and Mrs Bailey, and the latter's sister, Miss Atkinson, from 1890 to 1904.

Pond Cottages, *c.* 1900: an agreeable group of eighteenth- and nineteenth-century cottages bordering the Mill Pond.

A view of Sydenham Hill station, *c.* 1925, taken from the London platform and looking towards the Penge tunnel. The line was built by the London, Chatham and Dover Railway in 1863. The spire of St Stephen's Church can be seen on the left. It was built in 1867–8 to the designs of Charles Barry Jnr.

The southern end of Lordship Lane, *c.* 1910, showing a tram with the Grove Tavern in the background. This was the site of an eighteenth-century spa.

The Grove Tavern, 1950. Many pubs, including this one, were rebuilt in Tudor style between the wars.

Cox's Walk, Dulwich Common, *c.* 1907. John Cox, a vintner, acquired the lease of the Green Man (later the Grove Tavern) at the beginning of the eighteenth century. He laid out the walk to connect with Sydenham Hill.

A view over the south-eastern corner of Dulwich towards St Peter's Church, *c.* 1905.

# EAST DULWICH

*Barry Road, c. 1905.*

Dulwich Hospital from an architect's drawing, *c.* 1887. The hospital was built for St Saviour's Union, a Poor Law body which operated in Southwark and Walworth. It became a general hospital after the First World War.

Dulwich Hospital from East Dulwich Grove, *c.* 1905.

# NUNHEAD
# AND THE
# CEMETERIES

*The Old Nun's Head, Nunhead Green, c. 1930. The pub was rebuilt about five years later.*

The Nunhead Band of Hope, a temperance organization, 1917.

Nunhead Football Club, *c.* 1930. It was a very successful club in the Isthmian League between the wars. It was formed in 1888 and occupied Brown's Ground near Ivydale Road from 1907.

The workhouse in Gordon Road, showing the grilles through which the inmates had to put crushed stones.

Nunhead Cemetery, c. 1895, showing the road from the main entrance to the Anglican chapel. The cemetery had opened in 1840 and was run by the company which also owned Highgate Cemetery.

The chapel of Camberwell New Cemetery, Honor Oak, which opened in 1927. Sir Aston Webb was the chapel's architect.

Camberwell Old Cemetery's gates, Forest Hill, c. 1900. This cemetery had opened in 1856 and superseded St Giles's churchyard as the main local burial ground.

# THE WORLD WARS

*The grave of Able Seaman Albert Edward McKenzie VC,
in Camberwell Old Cemetery. He won his VC while
serving on HMS Vindictive in the storming of the mole
at Zeebrugge on 22–23 April 1918. He died of
influenza in the same year.*

Women delivering coke from the South Metropolitan Gas Works during the First World War. Women were recruited into many occupations for the first time as a result of the wartime labour shortage.

Military horses being kept in Lyndhurst Road (now Lyndhurst Way), 1915, to avoid infection at Gordon's Brewery.

Bomb damage at the junction of Albany Road and Calmington Road after a Zeppelin raid which killed twelve people on the night of 19/20 October 1917.

A plaque was erected in Calmington Road to commemorate the incident described above; it is seen here in 1977. The site is now part of Burgess Park.

Camberwell Town Hall on Peace Day, 19 July 1919. Peace Day followed the signing of the Treaty of Versailles on 28 June. The lamps shown here took five men twenty minutes to light.

An Air Raid Precautions rally at Camberwell Green, 14 May 1939. The expectation of war was growing rapidly by then.

Severe bomb damage to a block of the London County Council's flats in Peckham, autumn 1940.

The destruction of St Mary Magdalene's Church, St Mary's Road, Peckham, 1940. The church had been built in 1839–41 by Robert Palmer Browne. A new building has since taken its place.

A Victory party in Geldart Road, Peckham, 1945.

# ROYAL
# OCCASIONS

*Queen Elizabeth the Queen Mother visiting 238 Croxted Road on 9 July 1956. The Queen Mother has visited a number of private gardens in the borough over the years.*

Camberwell Green *en fête* for King Edward VII's visit on 20 July 1909. The sense of national and civic pride was very strong in that period. The view is from the foot of Denmark Hill, looking towards Camberwell Church Street. The Tiger public house (now the Silver Buckle) can be seen in the background on the right. 'All's Well' was the motto of Camberwell Borough Council.

King Edward VII and Queen Alexandra driving through Camberwell on Tuesday, 20 July 1909, on their way to lay the foundation stone of King's College Hospital at Denmark Hill.

King George V and Queen Mary visited Camberwell Green at the time of the Silver Jubilee, 18 May 1935. They alighted to receive addresses from the representatives of the South London boroughs.

Bunting in Troy Town, Peckham, for King George V's Silver Jubilee in 1935. Troy Town as a name has traditionally referred to a maze.

Spectators waiting at Camberwell Green for Queen Elizabeth II's Coronation drive in 1953. The view shows the junction of Camberwell New Road and Denmark Hill, looking across to the Silver Buckle public house.

Queen Elizabeth II coming down Denmark Hill on her Coronation drive, 9 June 1953.

# ACKNOWLEDGEMENTS

Acknowledgement is gladly made to Mr W.W. Marshall and Mr John Beasley for valuable information on the history of Peckham; to Mr Tony Wilson, editor of the *Camberwell Quarterly*, for bringing to my attention many matters of local interest; to Mr Brian Green for information on Dulwich; and to Miss Mary Boast for help over many years on a wide range of historical subjects. Almost all the pictures belong to the Southwark Local Studies Library and are reproduced by kind permission of Mrs Janice Brooker, Local Studies Librarian in 1994 5, and of her successor, Mr Len Reilly.